AIR FRYER BOOK

Easy and Appetizing Recipes for Light and Healthy Eating

PAUL GORDAN

Disclaimer Notice:

Please note the information contained within this document is for educational and entertainment purposes only. All effort has been executed to present accurate, up to date, and reliable, complete information. No warranties of any kind are declared or implied. Readers acknowledge that the author is not engaging in the rendering of legal, financial, medical or professional advice. The content within this book has been derived from various sources. Please consult a licensed professional before attempting any techniques outlined in this book.

By reading this document, the reader agrees that under no circumstances is the author responsible for any losses, direct or indirect, which are incurred as a result of the use of information contained within this document, including, but not limited to, errors, omissions, or inaccuracies.

Table of Contents

Sommario

Introduction

What is an air fryer?

Is an appliance that typically has an egg shape, more or less square, with a removable basket on which you put the food to be cooked. It takes advantage of the concept of air cooking at high temperatures that reach up to 200 ° allowing a healthy "frying-not-frying" of fresh foods. Abandon, then, the thought of frying during which the food is immersed in a lot of oil because the number of oil used inside the air fryer could be as little as a couple of teaspoons of spray. True frying in plenty of boiling oil is almost as "dangerous", especially in case you abuse it or don't pay proper attention. In the air fryer, the oil never reaches the smoke point and is therefore non-toxic.

Hot air, which reaches high temperatures, circulates inside the chamber of the air fryer allowing the food to be cooked evenly both externally and internally. This way you will cook meat, fish, vegetables, and thousands of other dishes in no time - in short, you can make many recipes with the air fryer. Meat cooked in an air fryer is juicy, tender, and soft, excess fat drips down and does not remain inside the meat giving it exceptional flavor.

The air fryer also works as an oven and grill...

The air fryer is quite different and in addition to its main purpose, the air cooking of food for a light and healthy fried food, it is also an appliance that serves as an oven for gratin for different recipes, pasta dishes, vegetables, to cook cakes and pies of all kinds, muffins, buns, pizzas. It has been shown that in the best performing models, the air fryer eliminates excess fat, even up to 50%, without altering the flavor of foods, giving the right crispness typical of fried foods.

Which air fryer to choose to buy?

For the choice of air fryer, the advice could also be an honest product to solicit better and better results. A high-quality product returns a product of equal quality. It would therefore be fair to consider spending slightly more for a much better-performing air fryer that also has better quality materials. However, depending on your needs, there are now many excellent products that are affordable for everyone.

Now you simply need to take a look inside the air fryer recipes. They are all proven, safe and excellent recipes!

Chicken

Chicken Alfredo with Mushrooms

(Ready in about 15 minutes | Servings 3)

334 Calories; 15.1g Fat; 13.4g Carbs; 36g Protein; 7.5g Sugars

Ingredients:

1 pound chicken breasts, boneless

1 medium onion, quartered

1 teaspoon butter, melted

1/2 pound mushrooms, cleaned

12 ounces Alfredo sauce

Salt and black pepper, to taste

Directions:

Start by preheating your Air Fryer to 380 degrees F. Then, place the chicken and onion in the cooking basket. Drizzle with melted butter. Cook in the preheated Air Fryer for 6 minutes. Add in the mushrooms and continue to cook for 5 to 6 minutes more.

Slice the chicken into strips. Chop the mushrooms and onions; stir in the Alfredo sauce. Salt and pepper to taste.

Serve with hot cooked fettuccine. Bon appétit!

Sticky Exotic Chicken Drumettes

(Ready in about 25 minutes | Servings 4)
317 Calories; 12.5g Fat; 11.5g Carbs; 38.4g Protein; 10.1g Sugars

Ingredients:

1tablespoons peanut oil

2 tablespoons honey

1 tablespoon tamari sauce

1 tablespoon yellow mustard

1 clove garlic, peeled and minced

2tablespoons fresh orange juice

½ teaspoon sambal oelek

1 ½ pounds chicken drumettes, bone-in

Salt and ground white pepper, to taste

¼ cup chicken broth

½ cup raw onion rings, for garnish

Directions:

Start by preheating your Air Fryer to 380 degrees F.

Line the cooking basket with parchment paper. Lightly grease the parchment paper with 1 tablespoon of peanut oil.

In a mixing bowl, thoroughly combine the remaining 1 tablespoon of oil, honey, tamari sauce, mustard, garlic, orange juice, and sambal oelek. Whisk to combine well.

Arrange the chicken drumettes in the prepared cooking basket. Season with salt and white pepper.

Spread 1/2 of the honey mixture evenly all over each breast. Pour in the chicken broth. Cook for 12 minutes.

Turn them over, add the remaining 1/2 of the honey mixture, and cook an additional 10 minutes.

Garnish with onion rings and serve immediately.

Thanksgiving Turkey Tenderloin with Gravy

(Ready in about 40 minutes | Servings 4)
374 Calories; 8.1g Fat; 20.5g Carbs; 52g Protein; 10.2g Sugars

Ingredients:
2 ½ pounds turkey tenderloin, sliced into pieces
1/2 head of garlic, peeled and halved
1 dried marjoram
Sea salt and ground black pepper, to taste
1 teaspoon cayenne pepper Gravy:
3 cups vegetable broth
1/3 cup all-purpose flour
Sea salt and ground black pepper, to taste

Directions:
Start by preheating your Air Fryer to 350 degrees F.

Rub the turkey tenderloins with garlic halves; add marjoram, salt, black pepper, and cayenne pepper.

Cook the turkey tenderloins at 350 degrees F for 30 minutes or until an instant-read thermometer inserted into the center of the breast reaches 165 degrees F; flip them over halfway through.

In a saucepan, place the drippings from the roasted turkey. Add 1 cup of broth and 1/6 cup of flour to the pan; whisk until it makes a smooth paste.

Once it gets a golden brown color, add the rest of the chicken broth and flour. Sprinkle with salt and pepper to taste.

Let it simmer over medium heat, stirring constantly for 6 to 7 minutes. Serve with warm turkey tenderloin and enjoy!

Chicken Taquitos with Homemade Guacamole

(Ready in about 35 minutes | Servings 4)
512 Calories; 35.2g Fat; 15.9g Carbs; 34.9g Protein; 4.7g Sugars

Ingredients:

1 tablespoon peanut oil

1 pound chicken breast

Seasoned salt and ground black pepper, to taste

1 teaspoon chili powder

1 teaspoon garlic powder

1 teaspoon ground cumin

1 cup Colby cheese, shredded

8 corn tortillas 1/2 cup sour cream

Guacamole:

1 ripe avocado, pitted and peeled

1 tomato, crushed

½ onion, finely chopped

1 tablespoon fresh cilantro, chopped

1 chili pepper, seeded and minced

1 teaspoon fresh garlic, minced

1 lime, juiced

Sea salt and black pepper, to taste

Directions:

Start by preheating your Air Fryer to 370 degrees F.

Drizzle the peanut oil all over the chicken breast. Then, rub the chicken breast with salt, black pepper, chili powder, garlic powder, and ground cumin. Cook in the preheated Air Fryer approximately 15 minutes. Turn them over and cook an additional 8 minutes.

Then, increase the temperature to 380 degrees F.

Divide the roasted chicken and cheese between tortillas. Now, roll up the tortilla and transfer them to the lightly greased cooking basket. Spritz a nonstick cooking spray over the tortillas.

Cook approximately 10 minutes, turning them over halfway through. Mash the avocado with a fork and add the remaining ingredients for the guacamole. Serve the chicken taquitos with the guacamole sauce and sour cream. Enjoy!

Easy Ritzy Chicken Nuggets

(Ready in about 20 minutes | Servings 4)
355 Calories; 20.1g Fat; 5.3g Carbs; 36.6g Protein; 0.2g Sugars

Ingredients:
1 ½ pounds chicken tenderloins, cut into small pieces
½ teaspoon garlic salt
½ teaspoon cayenne pepper
¼ teaspoon black pepper, freshly cracked
4 tablespoons olive oil
1/3 cup saltines (e.g. Ritz crackers), crushed
4 tablespoons Parmesan cheese, freshly grated

Directions:
Start by preheating your Air Fryer to 390 degrees F.

Season each piece of the chicken with garlic salt, cayenne pepper, and black pepper.

In a mixing bowl, thoroughly combine the olive oil with crushed saltines. Dip each piece of chicken in the cracker mixture.

Finally, roll the chicken pieces over the Parmesan cheese. Cook for 8 minutes, working in batches.

Later, if you want to warm the chicken nuggets, add them to the basket and cook for 1 minute more. Serve with French fries, if desired.

Pork

Delicious Chifa Chicharonnes

(Ready in about 1 hour 10 minutes | Servings 3)
415 Calories; 40g Fat; 5.3g Carbs; 7.3g Protein; 3.6g Sugars

Ingredients:
½ pound pork belly
1 cloves garlic, chopped
1 rosemary sprig, crushed
1 thyme sprig, crushed
1 teaspoon coriander
3 tablespoons kecap manis
Salt and red pepper, to taste

Directions:
Put the pork belly, rind side up, in the cooking basket; add in the garlic, rosemary, thyme and coriander.

Cook in the preheated Air Fryer at 350 degrees F for 20 minutes; turn it over and cook an additional 20 minutes.

Turn the temperature to 400 degrees F, rub the pork belly with the kecap manis and sprinkle with salt and red pepper. Continue to cook for 15 to 20 minutes more.

Let it rest on a wire rack for 10 minutes before slicing and serving. Enjoy!

Pigs in a Blanket with a Twist

(Ready in about 15 minutes | Servings 4)
589 Calories; 40g Fat; 40.1g Carbs; 16.8g Protein; 7g Sugars

Ingredients:

12 refrigerator biscuits

8 hot dogs, cut into 3 pieces

1 egg yolk

2 tablespoons poppy seeds

1 tablespoon oregano

Directions:

Flatten each biscuit slightly; cut in half.

Now, mix the egg yolk with the poppy seeds and oregano.

Wrap the biscuits around the hot dog pieces sealing the edges and brushing with the egg mixture to adhere.

Bake in the preheated Air Fryer at 395 degrees F for 8 minutes, Enjoy!

Pork Cutlets with a Twist

(Ready in about 1 hour 20 minutes | Servings 2)
579 Calories; 19.4g Fat; 50g Carbs; 49.6g Protein; 2.2g Sugars

Ingredients:

1 cup water
1 cup red wine
1 tablespoon sea salt
2 pork cutlets
½ cup all-purpose flour
1 teaspoon shallot powder
½ teaspoon porcini powder
Sea salt and ground black pepper, to taste
1 egg
¼ cup yogurt
1 teaspoon brown mustard
1 cup tortilla chips, crushed

Directions:

In a large ceramic dish, combine the water, wine and salt. Add the pork cutlets and put for 1 hour in the refrigerator.

In a shallow bowl, mix the flour, shallot powder, porcini powder, salt, and ground pepper. In another bowl, whisk the eggs with yogurt and mustard.

In a third bowl, place the crushed tortilla chips.

Dip the pork cutlets in the flour mixture and toss evenly; then, in the egg mixture. Finally, roll them over the crushed tortilla chips.

Spritz the bottom of the cooking basket with cooking oil. Add the breaded pork cutlets and cook at 395 degrees F and for 10 minutes. Flip and cook for 5 minutes more on the other side. Serve warm.

Rustic Pizza with Ground Pork

(Ready in about 30 minutes | Servings 4)
529 Calories; 9.6g Fat; 65.5g Carbs; 37.9g Protein; 0.9g Sugars

Ingredients:

1 (10-count) can refrigerator biscuits

4 tablespoons tomato paste

1 tablespoon tomato ketchup

2 teaspoons brown mustard

½ cup ground pork

½ cup ground beef sausage

1 red onion, thinly sliced

½ cup mozzarella cheese, shredded

Directions:

Spritz the sides and bottom of a baking pan with a nonstick cooking spray.

Press five biscuits into the pan. Brush the top of biscuit with 2 tablespoons of tomato paste.

Add 1/2 tablespoon of ketchup, 1 teaspoon of mustard, 1/4 cup of ground pork, 1/4 cup of beef sausage. Top with 1/2 of the red onion slices.

Bake in the preheated Air Fryer at 360 degrees F for 10 minutes.

Top with 1/4 cup of mozzarella cheese and bake another 5 minutes.

Repeat the process with the second pizza. Slice the pizza into halves, serve and enjoy!

Chinese Five-Spice Pork Ribs

(Ready in about 35 minutes | Servings 3)
591 Calories; 25g Fat; 6.3g Carbs; 73g Protein; 3.1g Sugars

Ingredients:
1 ½ pounds country-style pork ribs
1 teaspoon mustard powder
1 teaspoon cumin powder
1 teaspoon shallot powder
1 tablespoon Five-spice powder
Coarse sea salt and ground black pepper
1 teaspoon sesame oil
2 tablespoons soy sauce

Directions:
Toss the country-style pork ribs with spices and sesame oil and transfer them to the Air Fryer cooking basket.

Cook at 360 degrees F for 20 minutes; flip them over and continue to cook an additional 14 to 15 minutes.

Drizzle with soy sauce just before serving. Bon appétit!

Beef

Dad's Barbecued Ribs

(Ready in about 20 minutes + marinating time | Servings 3)
566 Calories; 45g Fat; 18g Carbs; 25.7g Protein; 10.3g Sugars

Ingredients:
1 pound beef ribs
1/4 cup ketchup
1/4 cup tequila
1 tablespoon brown mustard
1 tablespoon brown sugar
2 tablespoons soy sauce1/2 red onion, sliced
2 garlic cloves, pressed

Directions:
Cut the ribs into serving size portions and transfer them to a ceramic dish. Add in the remaining ingredients, cover and allow it to marinate in your refrigerator overnight.

Discard the marinade. Grill in the preheated Air Fryer at 400 degrees F for 10 minutes. Turn them over and continue to cook for 10 minutes more.

Meanwhile, make the sauce by warming the marinade ingredients in a nonstick pan. Spoon over the warm ribs and serve immediately.

Burgers with Caramelized Onions

(Ready in about 30 minutes | Servings 4)
475 Calories; 21.1g Fat; 33.3g Carbs; 36.2g Protein; 6.1g Sugars

Ingredients:

1 pound ground beef

Salt and ground black pepper, to taste

1 teaspoon garlic powder

½ teaspoon cumin powder

1 tablespoon butter

1 red onion, sliced

1 teaspoon brown sugar

1 tablespoon balsamic vinegar

1 tablespoon vegetable stock

4 hamburger buns

8 tomato slices

4 teaspoons mustard

Directions:

Start by preheating your Air Fryer to 370 degrees F. Spritz the cooking basket with nonstick cooking oil.

Mix the ground beef with salt, pepper, garlic powder, and cumin powder. Shape the meat mixture into four patties and transfer them to the preheated Air Fryer.

Cook for 10 minutes; turn them over and cook on the other side for 8 to 10 minutes more.

While the burgers are frying, melt the butter in a pan over medium-high heat. Then, add the red onion and sauté for 4 minutes or until soft.

Add the brown sugar, vinegar, and stock and cook for 2 to 3 minute more.

To assemble your burgers, add the beef patties to the hamburger buns. Top with the caramelized onion, tomato, and mustard. Serve immediately and enjoy!

Sunday Beef Schnitzel

(Ready in about 15 minutes | Servings 2)
501 Calories; 20.1g Fat; 24.1g Carbs; 54.3g Protein; 2g Sugars

Ingredients:

1 beef schnitzel
Salt and black pepper, to taste
2 ounces all-purpose flour
1 egg, beaten
½ cup breadcrumbs
½ teaspoon paprika
1 teaspoon olive oil
½ lemon, cut into wedges to serve

Directions:

Pat the beef dry and generously season it with salt and black pepper.
Add the flour to a rimmed plate. Place the egg in a shallow bowl and
mix the breadcrumbs and paprika in another bowl.
Dip the meat in the flour first, then the egg, then the
paprika/breadcrumb mixture. Drizzle olive oil over each beef
schnitzel.
Cook in the preheated Air Fryer at 390 degrees F for about 10
minutes, flipping the meat halfway through the cooking time. Bon
appétit!

Beef Nuggets with Cheesy Mushrooms

(Ready in about 25 minutes | Servings 4)
355 Calories; 15.7g Fat; 13.6g Carbs; 39.8g Protein; 3.4g Sugars

Ingredients:

1 eggs, beaten

4 tablespoons yogurt

1 cup tortilla chips, crushed

1 teaspoon dry mesquite flavored seasoning mix

Coarse salt and ground black pepper, to taste

½ teaspoon onion powder

1 pound cube steak, cut into bite-size pieces

1 pound button mushrooms

1 cup Swiss cheese, shredded

Directions:

In a shallow bowl, beat the eggs and yogurt. In a resealable bag, mix the tortilla chips, mesquite seasoning, salt, pepper, and onion powder.

Dip the steak pieces in the egg mixture; then, place in the bag, and shake to coat on all sides.

Cook at 400 degrees F for 14 minutes, flipping halfway through the cooking time.

Add the mushrooms to the lightly greased cooking basket. Top with shredded Swiss cheese.

Bake in the preheated Air Fryer at 400 degrees F for 5 minutes.

Serve with the beef nuggets. Bon appétit!

BBQ Glazed Beef Riblets

(Ready in about 15 minutes + marinating time | Servings 3)
258 Calories; 9.5g Fat; 10.4g Carbs; 32.7g Protein; 5.3g Sugars

Ingredients:
1 pound beef riblets

Sea salt and red pepper, to taste

¼ cup tomato paste

¼ cup Worcestershire sauce

1 tablespoons hot sauce

1 tablespoon oyster sauce

2 tablespoons rice vinegar

1 tablespoon stone-ground mustard

Directions:
Combine all ingredients in a glass dish, cover and marinate at least 2 hours in your refrigerator.

Discard the marinade and place riblets in the Air Fryer cooking basket.

Cook in the preheated Air Fryer at 360 degrees F for 12 minutes, shaking the basket halfway through to ensure even cooking.

Heat the reserved marinade in a small skillet over a moderate flame; spoon the glaze over the riblets and serve immedia

Fish

Haddock Steaks with Decadent Mango Salsa

(Ready in about 15 minutes | Servings 2)
411 Calories; 25.5g Fat; 18.4g Carbs; 26.3g Protein; 14g Sugars

Ingredients:
1 haddock steaks
1 teaspoon butter, melted
1 tablespoon white wine
Sea salt and ground black pepper, to taste
Mango salsa:
½ mango, diced
¼ cup red onion, chopped
1 chili pepper, deveined and minced

1 teaspoon cilantro, chopped
2 tablespoons fresh lemon juice

Directions:
Toss the haddock with butter, wine, salt and black pepper.
Cook the haddock in your Air Fryer at 400 degrees F for 5 minutes.
Flip the haddock and cook on the other side for 5 minutes more.
Meanwhile, make the mango salsa by mixing all ingredients. Serve the warm haddock with the chilled mango salsa and enjoy

Snapper Casserole with Gruyere Cheese

(Ready in about 25 minutes | Servings 4)
406 Calories; 19.9g Fat; 9.3g Carbs; 46.4g Protein; 4.5g Sugars

Ingredients:
2 tablespoons olive oil

1 shallot, thinly sliced

2 garlic cloves, minced

1 ½ pounds snapper fillets

Sea salt and ground black pepper, to taste

1 teaspoon cayenne pepper

½ teaspoon dried basil

½ cup tomato puree

½ cup white wine

1 cup Gruyere cheese, shredded

Directions:
Heat 1 tablespoon of olive oil in a saucepan over medium-high heat.
Now, cook the shallot and garlic until tender and aromatic.

Preheat your Air Fryer to 370 degrees F.

Grease a casserole dish with 1 tablespoon of olive oil. Place the
snapper fillet in the casserole dish. Season with salt, black pepper,
and cayenne pepper. Add the sautéed shallot mixture.

Add the basil, tomato puree and wine to the casserole dish. Cook for
10 minutes in the preheated Air Fryer.

Top with the shredded cheese and cook an additional 7 minutes.
Serve immediately.

Classic Fish Tacos

(Ready in about 15 minutes | Servings 3)
266 Calories; 10.8g Fat; 17.3g Carbs; 25.7g Protein; 2.6g Sugars

Ingredients:
1 pound codfish
1 tablespoon olive oil
1 teaspoon Cajun spice mix
Salt and red pepper, to taste
3 corn tortillas
1/2 avocado, pitted and diced
1 cup purple cabbage
1 jalapeño, minced

Directions:
Pat the codfish dry with paper towels; toss the codfish with olive oil, Cajun spice mix, salt and black pepper.
Cook your codfish at 400 degrees F for 5 to 6 minutes. Then, turn the fish over and cook on the other side for 6 minutes until they are opaque.
Let the fish rest for 5 minutes before flaking with a fork.
Assemble the tacos: place the flaked fish over warmed tortillas; top with avocado, purple cabbage and minced jalapeño. Enjoy!

Italian-Style Crab Bruschetta

(Ready in about 15 minutes | Servings 2)
458 Calories; 32.6g Fat; 15.4g Carbs; 25g Protein; 3.3g Sugars

Ingredients:

4 slices sourdough bread

2 tablespoons tomato ketchup

4 tablespoons mayonnaise

1 teaspoon fresh rosemary, chopped

8 ounces lump crabmeat

1 teaspoon granulated garlic

2 tablespoons shallots, chopped

4 tablespoons mozzarella cheese, crumbled

Directions:

Place the slices of sourdough bread on a flat surface.

In a mixing bowl, thoroughly combine the tomato ketchup, mayo, rosemary, crabmeat, garlic, and shallots.

Divide the crabmeat mixture between the slices of bread. Top with mozzarella cheese.

Bake in the preheated Air Fryer at 370 degrees F for 10 minutes. Bon appétit!

Dijon Catfish with Eggplant Sauce

(Ready in about 30 minutes | Servings 3)
336 Calories; 16.9g Fat; 18.6g Carbs; 28.2g Protein; 12.1g Sugars

Ingredients:

1 pound catfish fillets
Sea salt and ground black pepper, to taste
¼ cup Dijon mustard
1 tablespoon honey
1 tablespoon white vinegar
1 pound eggplant, 1 ½-inch cubes
2 ablespoons olive oil
1 tablespoon tahini
½ teaspoon garlic, minced
1 tablespoon parsley, chopped

Directions:

Pat the catfish dry with paper towels and generously season with salt and black pepper.

In a small mixing bowl, thoroughly combine Dijon mustard, honey and vinegar.

Cook the fish in your Air Fryer at 400 degrees F for 5 minutes. Turn the fish over and brush with the Dijon mixture; continue to cook for a further 5 minutes.

Then, set your Air Fryer to 400 degrees F. Add the eggplant chunks to the cooking basket and cook for 15 minutes, shaking the basket occasionally to ensure even cooking.

Transfer the cooked eggplant to a bowl of your food processor; stir in the remaining ingredients and blitz until everything is well blended and smooth.

Serve the warm catfish with the eggplant sauce on the side. Bon appétit!

Vegetable and Side Dishes

Roasted Chermoula Parsnip

(Ready in about 20 minutes | Servings 3)
201 Calories; 8.7g Fat; 30g Carbs; 2.4g Protein; 8.5g Sugars

Ingredients:

1 pound parsnip, trimmed, peeled and cut into 1/2 inch pieces
1 tablespoon fresh parsley leaves
1 tablespoon fresh cilantro leaves
2 garlic cloves
Salt and black pepper, to taste
½ teaspoon cayenne pepper
1 teaspoon ground cumin
½ teaspoon ground coriander
½ teaspoon saffron strands
4 tablespoons extra-virgin olive oil
1 tablespoon freshly squeezed lemon juice

Directions:

Place your parsnips in the Air Fryer cooking basket; spritz the parsnip with a nonstick cooking oil.

Cook the parsnip in the preheated Air Fryer at 380 degrees F for 15 minutes, shaking the basket halfway through the cooking time to ensure even browning.

Add the remaining ingredients to a bowl of your food processor or blender. Blend until smooth and well combined.

Spoon the Chermoula dressing over roasted parsnip and serve. Bon appétit!

Sweet Potato and Chickpea Tacos

(Ready in about 15 minutes | Servings 4)
427 Calories; 26.6g Fat; 34.4g Carbs; 15.3g Protein; 4.5g Sugars

Ingredients:

2 cups sweet potato puree
2 tablespoons butter, melted
14 ounces canned chickpeas, rinsed
1 cup Colby cheese, shredded
1 teaspoon garlic powder
1 teaspoon onion powder
Salt and freshly cracked black pepper, to taste
8 corn tortillas
¼ cup Pico de gallo
2 tablespoons fresh coriander, chopped

Directions:

Mix the sweet potatoes with the butter, chickpeas, cheese, garlic powder, onion powder, salt, black pepper.
Divide the sweet potato mixture between the tortillas. Bake in the preheated Air Fryer at 390 degrees F for 7 minutes.
Garnish with Pico de gallo and coriander. Bon appétit!

Roasted Veggies with Yogurt-Tahini Sauce

(Ready in about 20 minutes | Servings 4)
254 Calories; 17.2g Fat; 19.6g Carbs; 11.1g Protein; 8.1g Sugars

Ingredients:
1 pound Brussels sprouts
1 pound button mushrooms
2 tablespoons olive oil
½ teaspoon white pepper
½ teaspoon dried dill weed
½ teaspoon cayenne pepper
½ teaspoon celery seeds
½ teaspoon mustard seeds
Salt, to taste
Yogurt Tahini Sauce:
1 cup plain yogurt
2 heaping tablespoons tahini paste
1 tablespoon lemon juice
1 tablespoon extra-virgin olive oil
1/2 teaspoon Aleppo pepper, minced

Directions:
Toss the Brussels sprouts and mushrooms with olive oil and spices. Preheat your Air Fryer to 380 degrees F.
Add the Brussels sprouts to the cooking basket and cook for 10 minutes. Add the mushrooms, turn the temperature to 390 degrees and cook for 6 minutes more. While the vegetables are cooking, make the sauce by whisking all ingredients. Serve the warm vegetables with the sauce on the side. Bon appétit!

Spanish Patatas Bravas

(Ready in about 15 minutes | Servings 3)
166 Calories; 3.9g Fat; 32g Carbs; 4.5g Protein; 3.3g Sugars

Ingredients:
1 pound russet potatoes, cut into 1-inch cubes
2 teaspoons canola oil
Salt and ground black pepper, to taste
1 cup tomatoes, crushed
1/2 teaspoon paprika
1/2 teaspoon chili powder
2 garlic cloves, crushed
A pinch of brown sugar

Directions:
Toss the potatoes with 1 teaspoon of oil, salt and black pepper.
Transfer the potato chunks to the lightly oiled Air Fryer cooking basket.
Cook the potatoes in your Air Fryer at 400 degrees F for 12 minutes total, shaking the basket halfway through the cooking time.
In the meantime, heat the remaining teaspoon of oil in a saucepan over medium-high heat. Once hot, stir in the other ingredients cook for 8 to 10 minutes until cooked through.
Spoon the sauce over roasted potatoes and serve immediately.
Enjoy!

Roasted Corn Salad

(Ready in about 15 minutes + chilling time | Servings 3)
205 Calories; 9.5g Fat; 27g Carbs; 7.5g Protein; 7.9g Sugars

Ingredients:

2 ears of corn, husked

3 tablespoons sour cream

1/4 cup plain yogurt

1 garlic clove, minced

1 jalapeño pepper, seeded and minced

1 tablespoon fresh lemon juice

Pink salt and white pepper, to your liking

1 shallot, chopped

2 bell peppers, seeded and thinly sliced

2 tablespoons fresh parsley, chopped

¼ cup Queso Fresco, crumbled

Directions:

Start by preheating the Air Fryer to 390 degrees F. Spritz the Air Fryer grill pan with cooking spray.

Place the corn on the grill pan and cook for 10 minutes, turning over halfway through the cooking time. Set aside.

Once the corn has cooled to the touch, use a sharp knife to cut off the kernels into a salad bowl.

While the corn is resting, whisk the sour cream, yogurt, garlic, jalapeño pepper, fresh lemon juice, salt, and white pepper.

Add the shallot, pepper, and parsley to the salad bowl and toss to combine well. Toss with the sauce and serve topped with cheese. Enjoy!

Snacks & Appetizer

Coconut Banana Chips

(Ready in about 10 minutes | Servings 2)
105 Calories; 3.9g Fat; 18.5g Carbs; 0.9g Protein; 10.2g Sugars

Ingredients:

1 large banana, peeled and sliced
1 teaspoon coconut oil
¼ teaspoon ground cinnamon
A pinch of coarse salt
2 tablespoons coconut flakes

Directions:

Toss the banana slices with the coconut oil, cinnamon and salt.
Transfer banana slices to the Air Fryer cooking basket.
Cook the banana slices at 375 degrees F for about 8 minutes, shaking the basket every 2 minutes.
Scatter coconut flakes over the banana slices and let banana chips cool slightly before serving. Bon appétit!

Party Chicken Pillows

(Ready in about 20 minutes | Servings 4)
245 Calories; 16.6g Fat; 10.1g Carbs; 14.8g Protein; 3.5g Sugars

Ingredients:
1 teaspoon olive oil
1 cup ground chicken
1 (8-ounces) can Pillsbury Crescent Roll dough
Sea salt and ground black pepper, to taste
1 teaspoon onion powder
½ teaspoon garlic powder
4 tablespoons tomato paste
4 ounces cream cheese, at room temperature
2 tablespoons butter, melted

Directions:
Heat the olive oil in a pan over medium-high heat. Then, cook the ground chicken until browned or about 4 minutes.

Unroll the crescent dough. Roll out the dough using a rolling pin; cut into 8 pieces.

Place the browned chicken, salt, black pepper, onion powder, garlic powder, tomato paste, and cheese in the center of each piece.

Fold each corner over the filling using wet hands. Press together to cover the filling entirely and seal the edges.

Now, spritz the bottom of the Air Fryer basket with cooking oil. Lay the chicken pillows in a single layer in the cooking basket. Drizzle the melted butter all over chicken pillows.

Bake at 370 degrees F for 6 minutes or until golden brown. Work in batches. Bon appétit!

Mini Plantain Cups

(Ready in about 10 minutes | Servings 3)
322 Calories; 7.1g Fat; 63g Carbs; 5.5g Protein; 20.1g Sugars

Ingredients:

1 blackened plantains, chopped
¼ cup all-purpose flour
½ cup cornmeal
½ cup milk
1 tablespoon coconut oil
1 teaspoon fresh ginger, peeled and minced
A pinch of salt
A pinch of ground cinnamon

Directions:

In a mixing bowl, thoroughly combine all ingredients until everything is well incorporated.

Spoon the batter into a greased mini muffin tin.

Bake the mini plantain cups in your Air Fryer at 330 degrees F for 6 to 7 minutes or until golden brown.

Bon appétit!

Bruschetta with Fresh Tomato and Basil

(Ready in about 15 minutes | Servings 3)
161 Calories; 5.5g Fat; 23.8g Carbs; 4.4g Protein; 4.5g Sugars

Ingredients:

½ Italian bread, sliced

1 garlic cloves, peeled

2 tablespoons extra-virgin olive oil

2 ripe tomatoes, chopped

1 teaspoon dried oregano

Salt, to taste

8 fresh basil leaves, roughly chopped

Directions:

Place the bread slices on the lightly greased Air Fryer grill pan. Bake at 370 degrees F for 3 minutes.

Cut a clove of garlic in half and rub over one side of the toast; brush with olive oil. Add the chopped tomatoes. Sprinkle with oregano and salt.

Increase the temperature to 380 degrees F. Cook in the preheated Air Fryer for 3 minutes more.

Garnish with fresh basil and serve. Bon appétit!

Homemade Apple Chips

(Ready in about 20 minutes | Servings 4)
92 Calories; 3.4g Fat; 16.4g Carbs; 1.3g Protein; 12g Sugars

Ingredients:
1 cooking apples, cored and thinly sliced
1 teaspoon peanut oil
¼ teaspoon ground cloves
¼ teaspoon ground cinnamon
1 tablespoon smooth peanut butter

Directions:
Toss the apple slices with the peanut oil.
Bake at 350 degrees F for 5 minutes; shake the basket to ensure even cooking and continue to cook an additional 5 minutes.
Spread each apple slice with a little peanut butter and sprinkle with ground cloves and cinnamon. Bon appétit!

Rice and Grains

Bacon and Cheese Sandwich

(Ready in about 15 minutes | Servings 1)
406 Calories; 26.2g Fat; 27g Carbs; 14.2g Protein; 8.3g Sugars

Ingredients:

1 slices whole-wheat bread

2 tablespoon ketchup

½ teaspoon Dijon mustard

1 ounces bacon, sliced

1 ounce cheddar cheese, sliced

Directions:

Spread the ketchup and mustard on a slice of bread. Add the bacon and cheese and top with another slice of bread.

Place your sandwich in the lightly buttered Air Fryer cooking basket. Now, bake your sandwich at 380 degrees F for 10 minutes or until the cheese has melted. Make sure to turn it over halfway through the cooking time.

Bon appétit!

Mexican Taco Bake

(Ready in about 40 minutes | Servings 4)
540 Calories; 29.5g Fat; 33.3g Carbs; 34.8g Protein; 7.2g Sugars

Ingredients:

1 tablespoon olive oil

¼ pound ground beef

½ pound ground pork

1 shallot, minced

1 garlic, minced

½ cup beef broth

1 bell pepper, seeded and chopped

1 Mexican chili pepper, seeded and minced

1 ½ cups tomato sauce

4 flour tortillas for fajitas

1 cup Mexican cheese blend, shredded

Directions:

Heat the olive oil in a heavy skillet over a moderate flame. Cook the ground meat with the shallots and garlic until no longer pink.

Then, add the beef broth, peppers, and tomato sauce to the skillet. Continue to cook on low heat for 3 minutes, stirring continuously.

Spritz a baking dish with nonstick cooking spray. Cut the tortillas in half; place 2 tortilla halves in the bottom of the baking dish.

Top with half of the meat mixture. Sprinkle with 1/2 cup of the cheese and the remaining tortilla halves. Top with the remaining meat mixture and cheese.

Cover with a piece of aluminum foil and bake in the preheated Air Fryer at 330 degrees F for 20 minutes. Remove the foil and bake for a further 12 minutes or until thoroughly heated. Enjoy!

Risotto Balls with Bacon and Corn

(Ready in about 30 minutes + chilling time | Servings 6)
435 Calories; 15.6g Fat; 47.4g Carbs; 23.3g Protein; 4.1g Sugars

Ingredients:

4 slices Canadian bacon

1 tablespoon olive oil

½ medium-sized leek, chopped

1 teaspoon fresh garlic, minced

Sea salt and freshly ground pepper, to taste

1 cup white rice

4 cups vegetable broth

1/3 cup dry white wine

2 tablespoons tamari sauce

1 tablespoon oyster sauce

1 tablespoon butter

1 cup sweet corn kernels

1 bell pepper, seeded and chopped

2 eggs lightly beaten

1 cup bread crumbs

1 cup parmesan cheese, preferably freshly grated

Directions:

Cook the Canadian bacon in a nonstick skillet over medium-high heat. Let it cool, finely chop and reserve.

Heat the olive oil in a saucepan over medium heat. Now, sauté the leeks and garlic, stirring occasionally, about 5 minutes. Add the salt and pepper.

Stir in the white rice. Continue to cook approximately 3 minutes or until translucent. Add the warm broth, wine, tamari sauce, and oyster sauce; cook until the liquid is absorbed.

Remove the saucepan from the heat; stir in the butter, corn, bell pepper, and reserved Canadian bacon. Let it cool completely. Then, shape the mixture into small balls.

In a shallow bowl, combine the eggs with the breadcrumbs and parmesan cheese. Dip each ball in the eggs/crumb mixture.

Cook in the preheated Air Fryer at 395 degrees F for 10 to 12 minutes, shaking the basket periodically. Serve warm.

Apple Cinnamon Rolls

(Ready in about 20 minutes / Servings 4)
268 Calories; 5.7g Fat; 50.1g Carbs; 5.2g Protein; 14.4g Sugars

Ingredients:
1 (10-ounces) can buttermilk biscuits
1 apple, cored and chopped
¼ cup powdered sugar
1 teaspoon cinnamon
1 tablespoon coconut oil, melted

Directions:
Line the bottom of the Air Fryer cooking basket with a parchment paper.

Separate the dough into biscuits and cut each of them into 2 layers. Mix the remaining ingredients in a bowl.

Divide the apple/cinnamon mixture between biscuits and roll them up. Brush the biscuits with coconut oil and transfer them to the Air Fryer cooking basket.

Cook the rolls at 330 degrees F for about 13 minutes, turning them over halfway through the cooking time. Bon appétit!

Stuffed French Toast

(Ready in about 15 minutes | Servings 3)
430 Calories; 24.1g Fat; 44.1g Carbs; 10.3g Protein; 24g Sugars

Ingredients:

6 slices of challah bread, without crusts
¼ cup Mascarpone cheese
3 tablespoons fig jam
1 egg
4 tablespoons milk
½ teaspoon grated nutmeg
1 teaspoon ground cinnamon
½ teaspoon vanilla paste
¼ cup butter, melted
½ cup brown sugar

Directions:

Spread the three slices of bread with the mascarpone cheese, leaving 1/2-inch border at the edges.

Spread the three slices of bread with 1/2 tablespoon of fig jam; then, invert them onto the slices with the cheese in order to make sandwiches.

Mix the egg, milk, nutmeg, cinnamon, and vanilla in a shallow dish. Dip your sandwiches in the egg mixture.

Cook in the preheated Air Fryer at 340 degrees F for 4 minutes. Dip in the melted butter, then, roll in the brown sugar. Serve warm.

Vegan

The Best Potato Fritters Ever

(Ready in about 55 minutes | Servings 3)
304 Calories; 6.5g Fat; 55.1g Carbs; 7.4g Protein; 2.6g Sugars

Ingredients:

3 medium-sized potatoes, peeled

1 tablespoon flax seeds, ground

½ cup plain flour

½ teaspoon cayenne pepper

¼ teaspoon dried dill weed

Sea salt and ground black pepper, to taste

1 tablespoon olive oil

1 tablespoon fresh chives, chopped

Directions:

Place your potatoes in the Air Fryer cooking basket and cook them at 400 degrees F for about 40 minutes, shaking the basket occasionally to promote even cooking. Mash your potatoes with a fork or potato masher.

Make a vegan egg by mixing 1 tablespoon of ground flax seeds with 1 ½ tablespoons of water. Let it stand for 5 minutes.

Stir in the mashed potatoes, flour and spices; form the mixture into equal patties and brush them with olive oil.

Cook your fritters at 390 degrees F for about 10 minutes, flipping them halfway through the cooking time.

Garnish with fresh, chopped chives and serve warm. Bon app

Garlic-Roasted Brussels Sprouts with Mustard

(Ready in about 20 minutes | Servings 3)
151 Calories; 9.6g Fat; 14.5g Carbs; 5.4g Protein; 3.4g Sugars

Ingredients:

1 pound Brussels sprouts, halved

2 tablespoons olive oil

Sea salt and freshly ground black pepper, to taste

2 garlic cloves, minced

1tablespoon Dijon mustard

Directions:

Toss the Brussels sprouts with the olive oil, salt, black pepper, and garlic.

Roast in the preheated Air Fryer at 380 degrees F for 15 minutes, shaking the basket occasionally.

Serve with Dijon mustard and enjoy!

Italian-Style Pasta Chips

(Ready in about 15 minutes | Servings 2)
224 Calories; 3.4g Fat; 43.4g Carbs; 6.1g Protein; 0.1g Sugars

Ingredients:

1 cup dry rice pasta

1 teaspoon olive oil

1 tablespoon nutritional yeast

½ teaspoon dried oregano

½ teaspoon dried basil

1 teaspoon dried parsley flakes

Kosher salt and ground black pepper, to taste

Directions:

Cook the pasta according to the manufacturer's instructions. Drain your pasta and toss it with the remaining ingredients.

Cook the pasta chips at 390 degrees F for about 10 minutes, shaking the cooking basket halfway through the cooking time.

The pasta chips will crisp up as it cools.

Serve with tomato ketchup if desired. Bon appétit!

Barbecue Roasted Almonds

(Ready in about 20 minutes | Servings 6)
340 Calories; 30.1g Fat; 11.5g Carbs; 11.3g Protein; 2.3g Sugars

Ingredients:

1 ½ cups raw almonds
Sea salt and ground black pepper, to taste
¼ teaspoon garlic powder
¼ teaspoon mustard powder
½ teaspoon cumin powder
¼ teaspoon smoked paprika
1 tablespoon olive oil

Directions:

Toss all ingredients in a mixing bowl.
Line the Air Fryer basket with baking parchment. Spread out the coated almonds in a single layer in the basket.
Roast at 350 degrees F for 6 to 8 minutes, shaking the basket once or twice. Work in batches. Enjoy!

Warm Farro Salad with Roasted Tomatoes

(Ready in about 40 minutes | Servings 2)
452 Calories; 14.5g Fat; 72.9g Carbs; 7.7g Protein; 9.5g Sugars

Ingredients:

¾ cup farro

2 cups water

1 tablespoon sea salt

1 pound cherry tomatoes

2 spring onions, chopped

2 carrots, grated

2 heaping tablespoons fresh parsley leaves

2 tablespoons champagne vinegar

2 tablespoons white wine

2 tablespoons extra-virgin olive oil

1 teaspoon red pepper flakes

Directions:

Place the farro, water, and salt in a saucepan and bring it to a rapid boil. Turn the heat down to medium-low, and simmer, covered, for 30 minutes or until the farro has softened.

Drain well and transfer to an air fryer-safe pan.

Meanwhile, place the cherry tomatoes in the lightly greased Air Fryer basket. Roast at 400 degrees F for 4 minutes.

Add the roasted tomatoes to the pan with the cooked farro, Toss the salad ingredients with the spring onions, carrots, parsley, vinegar, white wine, and olive oil.

Bake at 360 degrees F an additional 5 minutes. Serve garnished with red pepper flakes and enjoy!

Dessert

Easy Monkey Rolls

(Ready in about 25 minutes | Servings 4)
432 Calories; 29.3g Fat; 40.1g Carbs; 4.1g Protein; 16.8g Sugars

Ingredients:

8 ounces refrigerated buttermilk biscuit dough

½ cup brown sugar

4 ounces butter, melted

¼ teaspoon grated nutmeg

½ teaspoon ground cinnamon

¼ teaspoon ground cardamom

Directions:

Spritz 4 standard-size muffin cups with a nonstick spray. Thoroughly combine the brown sugar with the melted butter, nutmeg, cinnamon and cardamom.

Spoon the butter mixture into muffins cups.

Separate the dough into biscuits and divide your biscuits between muffin cups.

Bake the Monkey rolls at 340 degrees F for about 15 minutes or until golden brown. Turn upside down just before serving. Bon appétit!

Rustic Baked Apples

(Ready in about 25 minutes | Servings 4)
211 Calories; 5.1g Fat; 45.5g Carbs; 2.6g Protein; 33.9g Sugars

Ingredients:

4 Gala apples

¼ cup rolled oats

¼ cup sugar

2 tablespoons honey

1/3 cup walnuts, chopped

1 teaspoon cinnamon powder

½ teaspoon ground cardamom

½ teaspoon ground cloves

2/3 cup water

Directions:

Use a paring knife to remove the stem and seeds from the apples, making deep holes.

In a mixing bowl, combine together the rolled oats, sugar, honey, walnuts, cinnamon, cardamom, and cloves.

Pour the water into an Air Fryer safe dish. Place the apples in the dish.

Bake at 340 degrees F for 17 minutes. Serve at room temperature.

Bon appétit!

Authentic Indian Gulgulas

(Ready in about 20 minutes | Servings 3)
252 Calories; 4.9g Fat; 43.8g Carbs; 7.9g Protein; 15.4g Sugars

Ingredients:

1 banana, mashed

¼ cup sugar

1 egg

½ teaspoon vanilla essence

¼ teaspoon ground cardamom

¼ teaspoon cinnamon

½ milk

¾ cup all-purpose flour

1 teaspoon baking powder

Directions:

In a mixing bowl, whisk the mashed banana with the sugar and egg; add the vanilla, cardamom, and cinnamon and mix to combine well. Gradually pour in the milk and mix again. Stir in the flour and baking powder. Mix until everything is well incorporated.

Drop a spoonful of batter onto the greased Air Fryer pan. Cook in the preheated Air Fryer at 360 degrees F for 5 minutes, flipping them halfway through the cooking time.

Repeat with the remaining batter and serve warm. Enjoy!

Bakery-Style Hazelnut Cookies

(Ready in about 20 minutes | Servings 6)

450 Calories; 28.6g Fat; 43.9g Carbs; 8.1g Protein; 17.5g Sugars

Ingredients:

1 ½ cups all-purpose flour

1 teaspoon baking soda

1 teaspoon fine sea salt

1 stick butter

1 cup brown sugar

2 teaspoons vanilla

1 eggs, at room temperature

1 cup hazelnuts, coarsely chopped

Directions:

Begin by preheating your Air Fryer to 350 degrees F.

Mix the flour with the baking soda, and sea salt.

In the bowl of an electric mixer, beat the butter, brown sugar, and vanilla until creamy. Fold in the eggs, one at a time, and mix until well combined.

Slowly and gradually, stir in the flour mixture. Finally, fold in the coarsely chopped hazelnuts.

Divide the dough into small balls using a large cookie scoop; drop onto the prepared cookie sheets. Bake for 10 minutes or until golden brown, rotating the pan once or twice through the cooking time. Work in batches and cool for a couple of minutes before removing to wire racks. Enjoy!

Mom's Orange Rolls

(Ready in about 1 hour 20 minutes | Servings 6)
365 Calories; 14.1g Fat; 51.9g Carbs; 7.3g Protein; 19.1g Sugars

Ingredients:

½ cup milk

¼ cup granulated sugar

1 tablespoon yeast

½ stick butter, at room temperature

1 egg, at room temperature

¼ teaspoon salt

2 cups all-purpose flour2 tablespoons fresh orange juice

Filling:

2 tablespoons butter

4 tablespoons white sugar

1 teaspoon ground star anise

¼ teaspoon ground cinnamon

1 teaspoon vanilla paste

½ cup confectioners' sugar

Directions:

Heat the milk in a microwave safe bowl and transfer the warm milk to the bowl of a stand electric mixer. Add the granulated sugar and yeast, and mix to combine well. Cover and let it sit until the yeast is foamy.

Then, beat the butter on low speed. Fold in the egg and mix again. Add salt and flour. Add the orange juice and mix on medium speed until a soft dough forms.

Knead the dough on a lightly floured surface. Cover it loosely and let it sit in a warm place about

1 hour or until doubled in size. Then, spritz the bottom and sides of a baking pan with cooking oil (butter flavored).

Roll your dough out into a rectangle. Spread 2 tablespoons of butter all over the dough. In a mixing dish, combine the white sugar, ground star anise, cinnamon, and vanilla; sprinkle evenly over the dough. Then, roll up your dough to form a log. Cut into 6 equal rolls and place them in the parchmentlined Air Fryer basket.

Bake at 350 degrees for 12 minutes, turning them halfway through the cooking time. Dust with confectioners' sugar and enjoy!

Other Air Fryer

Greek Fried Cheese Balls (Tirokroketes)

(Ready in about 40 minutes | Servings 3)
274 Calories; 17.3g Fat; 7.2g Carbs; 16.1g Protein; 2.4g Sugars

Ingredients:

4 ounces smoked gouda cheese, shredded
2 ounces feta cheese, crumbled
1 tablespoon all-purpose flour
1 egg, whisked
1tablespoon full-fat milk
½ cup bread crumbs

Directions:

In a bowl, mix all ingredients, except for the bread crumbs; cover the bowl with plastic wrap and transfer it to your refrigerator for 30 minutes.

Use about a spoonful of the mixture and roll it into a ball. Roll your balls into breadcrumbs and transfer them to a lightly greased cooking basket.

Cook cheese balls at 390 degrees F for about 7 minutes, shaking the basket halfway through the cooking time. Eat warm.

Classic Potato Latkes

(Ready in about 20 minutes | Servings 3)
279 Calories; 5.2g Fat; 48.4g Carbs; 9.1g Protein; 7.5g Sugars

Ingredients:

½ cup all-purpose flour

2 tablespoons matzo meal

1 potato, scrubbed and grated

1 small-sized sweet onion, finely chopped

1 egg, beaten

Coarse sea salt and ground black pepper, to taste

1 teaspoon chicken schmaltz, melted

Directions:

Thoroughly combine the flour, matzo meal, potato, onion and egg in a mixing bowl. Season with the salt and pepper to taste.

Drop the mixture in 2-tablespoon dollops into the cooking basket, flattening the tops with a wide spatula.

Drizzle each patty with the melted chicken schmaltz.

Cook your latkes in the preheated Air Fryer at 370 degrees F for 15 minutes or until thoroughly cooked and crispy.

Bon appétit!

Salted Pretzel Crescents

(Ready in about 20 minutes | Servings 4)
273 Calories; 16.3g Fat; 23.7g Carbs; 6.6g Protein; 4.4g Sugars

Ingredients:

1 can crescent rolls

10 cups water

½ cup baking soda

1 egg, whisked with 1 tablespoon water

1tablespoon poppy seeds

2tablespoons sesame seed

1 teaspoon coarse sea salt

Directions:

Unroll the dough onto your work surface; separate into 8 triangles.
In a large saucepan, bring the water and baking soda to a boil over
high heat.

Cook each roll for 30 seconds. Remove from the water using a
slotted spoon; place on a kitchen towel to drain.

Repeat with the remaining rolls. Now, brush the tops with the egg
wash; sprinkle each roll with the poppy seeds, sesame seed and
coarse sea salt. Cover and let rest for 10 minutes.

Arrange the pretzels in the lightly greased Air Fryer basket.

Bake in the preheated Air Fryer at 340 degrees for 7 minutes or until
golden brown. Bon appétit!

Red Currant Cupcakes

(Ready in about 20 minutes | Servings 3)
346 Calories; 8.5g Fat; 58.9g Carbs; 8.7g Protein; 22.2g Sugars

Ingredients:
1 cup all-purpose flour
½ cup sugar
1 teaspoon baking powder
A pinch of kosher salt
A pinch of grated nutmeg
¼ cup coconut, oil melted
1 egg
¼ cup full-fat coconut milk
¼ teaspoon ground cardamom
¼ teaspoon ground cinnamon
1 teaspoon vanilla extract
6 ounces red currants

Directions:
Mix the flour with the sugar, baking powder, salt, and nutmeg. In a separate bowl, whisk the coconut oil, egg, milk, cardamom, cinnamon, and vanilla.

Add the egg mixture to the dry ingredients; mix to combine well. Now, fold in the red currants; gently stir to combine. Scrape the batter into lightly greased 6 standard-size muffin cups.

Bake your cupcakes at 360 degrees F for 12 minutes or until the tops are golden brown. Sprinkle some extra icing sugar over the top of each muffin if desired. Enjoy!

Chive, Feta and Chicken Frittata

(Ready in about 10 minutes | Servings 4)
176 Calories; 7.7g Fat; 2.4g Carbs; 22.8g Protein; 1.5g Sugars

Ingredients:
1/3 cup Feta cheese, crumbled
1 teaspoon dried rosemary
½ teaspoon brown sugar
2t ablespoons fish sauce
1 ½ cup cooked chicken breasts, boneless and shredded
½ teaspoon coriander sprig, finely chopped
3 medium-sized whisked eggs
1/3 teaspoon ground white pepper
1 cup fresh chives, chopped
½ teaspoon garlic paste
Fine sea salt, to taste
Nonstick cooking spray

Directions:
Grab a baking dish that fit in your air fryer.
Lightly coat the inside of the baking dish with a nonstick cooking spray of choice. Stir in all ingredients, minus Feta cheese. Stir to combine well.
Set your machine to cook at 335 degrees for 8 minutes; check for doneness. Scatter crumbled Feta over the top and eat immediately!

CPSIA information can be obtained
at www.ICGtesting.com
Printed in the USA
BVHW092305270421
605945BV00010B/1279